CAPITAL!

Washington D.C. from A to Z

By Laura Krauss Melmed

Illustrated by Frané Lessac

HarperCollins*Publishers*

To Jewell Stoddard,
for helping Washington's children find joy in books,
and for helping me find my wings
—L.K.M.

For Cousin Ann
—F.L.

Capital! Washington D.C. from A to Z
Copyright © 2003 by Laura Krauss Melmed
Illustrations copyright © 2003 by Frané Lessac
Manufactured in China. All rights reserved.
www.harperchildrens.com

Library of Congress Cataloging-in-Publication Data
Melmed, Laura Krauss.
Capital! : Washington D.C. from A to Z / Laura Krauss Melmed ; illustrated by Frané Lessac.
p.   cm.
Summary: Rhyming text and illustrations present the sights of Washington, D.C., from A to Z.
ISBN 0-688-17561-9 — ISBN 0-688-17562-7 (lib. bdg.)
1. Washington (D.C.)—Juvenile literature.   2. English language—Alphabet—
Juvenile literature.   [1. Washington (D.C.)   2. Alphabet.]   I. Title: Washington D.C. from A to Z.
II. Lessac, Frané, ill.   III. Title.
F194.3 .M45   2003   2001039513   975.3[E]—dc21   CIP   AC

Typography by Stephanie Bart-Horvath
5   6   7   8   9   10
❖
First Edition

Welcome!

Imagine yourself on a journey. You have been driving on dusty roads all night. As the sun rises, you find yourself on a broad avenue lined with tall, leafy trees. Clear morning light gleams on white marble buildings. A grand, domed structure with shaded grounds stands before you.

A long time ago, on a trip from the southern part of the United States to the north, I rode through this beautiful scene in Washington, D.C. Several years later, I was lucky enough to move here.

Washington, D.C., is the capital of our country, headquarters for the president, Congress, and the Supreme Court. But since our government is a democracy, each of us plays an important part in it. So whether you live in Anchorage or Detroit, on a farm in Nebraska or a small town in Mississippi, Washington is yours to be proud of.

The places in *Capital!* range from inspirational sites like the Lincoln Memorial, to places of solemn importance like the Holocaust Memorial Museum, to popular spots like the National Zoo. All of them together make Washington a city like no other. If you have been to Washington, you can use this book as a remembrance of what you saw and did. If not, I hope that one day you will have the chance to visit or to live here, so that you can explore for yourself, from A to Z, your very special capital, Washington, D.C.

Laura Krauss Melmed

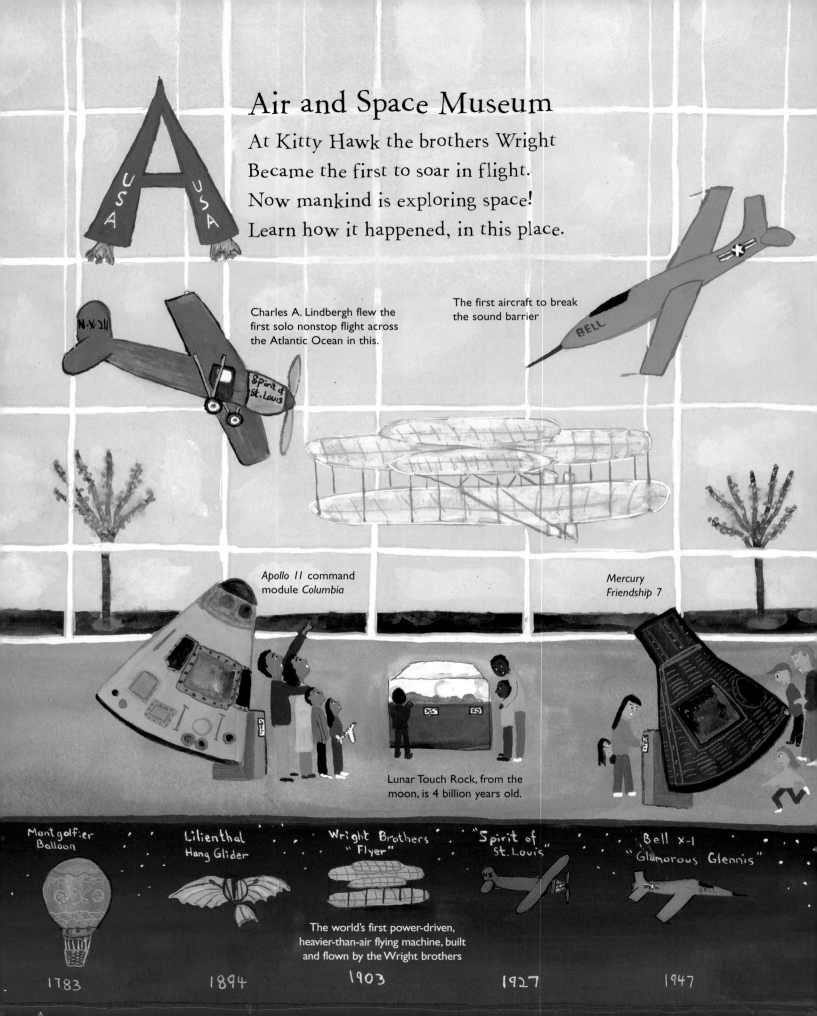

Air and Space Museum

At Kitty Hawk the brothers Wright
Became the first to soar in flight.
Now mankind is exploring space!
Learn how it happened, in this place.

Charles A. Lindbergh flew the first solo nonstop flight across the Atlantic Ocean in this.

The first aircraft to break the sound barrier

Apollo 11 command module *Columbia*

Mercury Friendship 7

Lunar Touch Rock, from the moon, is 4 billion years old.

Montgolfier Balloon

Lilienthal Hang Glider

Wright Brothers "Flyer"

"Spirit of St. Louis"

Bell X-1 "Glamorous Glennis"

The world's first power-driven, heavier-than-air flying machine, built and flown by the Wright brothers

1783   1894   1903   1927   1947

The Minuteman III is the cornerstone of our nation's land-based nuclear arsenal. It has a range of over 7,000 miles.

Kites were among the first man-made flying objects. The museum has kites presented by the Chinese Imperial Collection in 1876.

V-2 Rocket

Jupiter-C

Aerobee 150

Viking

UE

UNITED STA

Neil Armstrong's spacesuit from *Apollo 11*

"Mercury Friendship 7"

X-15

"Apollo 11"

"Apollo-Soyez"

"Endeavour 100"

USA

CGCP

e first American to orbit Earth aveled in this.

The first winged aircraft to fly higher than 100,000 feet. It once flew 67 miles high!

The first humans to walk on the moon rode in this command module.

Who knows what we'll be flying to space in the future?

1962

1967

1969

1975

2083

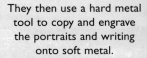

They then use a hard metal tool to copy and engrave the portraits and writing onto soft metal.

Engravers sketch the portraits and writing that appear on the bills.

The engraving is used to manufacture a metal printing plate with dozens of images of the bill.

Bureau of Engraving and Printing

They have a mission to fulfill
By printing every U.S. bill,
And so their motto is sincere,
For it proclaims,
"The buck starts here!"

The printing plates are covered with ink.

Using tremendous pressure, a high-speed press forces the plates against the paper.

FEDERAL RESERVE NOTE

THE UNITED STATES OF AMERICA

THIS NOTE IS LEGAL TENDER
FOR ALL DEBTS, PUBLIC AND PRIVATE

3

18061954

WASHINGTON, D.C.

ONE

Every bill has its own serial number.

B94305473

3

WASHINGTON

SERIES 2002

ONE DOLLAR

3

Federal Reserve Number appears four times on the bill.

Federal Reserve Seal

THE GREAT SEAL OF THE UNITED STATES
appears on the back of every dollar bill.

An Egyptian pyramid on the back of the seal represents strength and duration. The pyramid is unfinished to show that the United States will build and grow in the future.

NOVUS ORDO SECLORUM

The Eagle of Democracy on the face of the seal represents the branches of American government:

Head = the executive branch
Shield = the legislative branch
Tail feathers = the judicial branch

There is a portrait of a different famous person (generally a president) on each denomination:

$1   George Washington
$5   Abraham Lincoln
$10   Alexander Hamilton
$20   Andrew Jackson
$50   Ulysses S. Grant
$100   Benjamin Franklin

The bills are then cut apart, dried, and stored in vaults until they are sent to banks.

The printing process is called *intaglio*.

Almost $696 million of paper bills, called *currency*, is printed at the bureau every day.

Capitol

The House and Senate make their home
Beneath the Capitol's great dome.
The bills they vote upon each day
May soon be laws we must obey.

Congress, made up of senators and representatives, debates and passes our nation's new laws in the United States Capitol.

The bronze Statue of Freedom is a woman in flowing robes. In her left hand she holds a victory wreath and the shield of the United States with thirteen stripes representing the thirteen colonies. Her right hand rests on a sheathed sword.

The dome is made of cast iron and weighs almost *9 million* pounds!

The Capitol has about 540 rooms, 658 windows, and 850 doorways.

THE SENATE

A member of the Senate is called a senator. Senators are elected every six years. There are two senators from each state.

Visitors may sit in the *gallery* in both the House of Representatives and the Senate, to see and hear Congress at work.

Each senator has a desk. One desk is called the candy desk, and each new senator who uses it keeps the drawer filled with mints, hard candies, and chocolates.

THE HOUSE OF REPRESENTATIVES

A member of the House of Representatives is called a representative, a congressman, or a congresswoman. Representatives are elected every two years. The number of representatives from each state depends on the state's population.

The head of the House of Representatives is called the *Speaker*.

IN GOD WE TRUST

In the House Chamber, members may sit in any seat. But Democrats usually sit to the right of the Speaker and Republicans to the left.

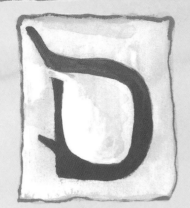

Declaration of Independence

On proud display for all to see
Are words that altered history
And helped to make a nation free,
Protecting life and liberty.

THE
DECLARATION OF INDEPENDENCE
THE
CONSTITUTION
OF THE
UNITED STATES OF AMERICA
AND THE
BILL OF RIGHTS

The original Declaration of Independence, the Constitution, and the Bill of Rights are displayed together in the Rotunda of the National Archives. They are under armed guard, and at night the documents are stored in special vaults to protect against theft and fire.

The name "United States of America" was used for the first time ever in the Declaration of Independence. The Declaration of Independence was signed on August 2, 1776. Thomas Jefferson was its author.

We hold these truths to be self-evident, that all men are created equal, that they are endowed by their Creator with certain unalienable Rights, that among these are Life, Liberty and the pursuit of Happiness.—That to secure these rights, Governments are instituted among Men, deriving their just powers from the consent of the governed,—That whenever any Form of Government becomes destructive of these ends, it is the Right of the People to alter or to abolish it, and to institute new Government, laying its foundation on such principles and organizing its powers in such form, as to them shall seem most likely to effect their Safety and Happiness.

Famous words from the Declaration of Independence

Embassy Row

From other countries, far and near,
Ambassadors are posted here
To help their governments convey
Their friendship to the U.S.A.

Diplomats from all over the world are sent to live in Washington to speak and listen on behalf of their governments. They work in buildings called embassies. More than 170 foreign countries currently have embassies in Washington.

Greece

Consulate of Greece

Massachusetts Avenue is nicknamed Embassy Row because many embassies are found here.

The head diplomat of each country is called an ambassador.

The FBI investigates certain types of crimes, such as violent crimes, crimes against civil rights, and terrorism.

In the FBI Crime Labs, scientists analyze evidence found at the scene of a crime, like bones, fabric, paint chips, and even insects.

The FBI's Ten Most Wanted!

Forensic scientists at the FBI can enlarge fingerprints found at a crime scene and search through their computer data banks to find a match.

Criminals nabbed by the FBI

Dogs who work for the FBI can detect a scent as far as a half-mile away. They are trained to sniff out bombs, drugs, or money.

From left to right: "Pretty Boy" Floyd, Clyde Barrow and Bonnie Parker, Al Capone, "Machine Gun" Kelly, "Baby Face" Nelson

Federal Bureau of Investigation

Who searches for the Ten Most Wanted
And faces terrorists, undaunted?
Who'll ambush the most clever spy
Or solve a crime? The FBI!

Gallaudet University

In eighteen hundred sixty-four,
President Lincoln signed a law
Providing higher education
For the nonhearing population.

American Sign Language, or ASL, is one way deaf people communicate. It uses hand signs as well as facial expressions and body postures. All students and teachers at Gallaudet must learn ASL.

Edward Gallaudet
1837–1917

Gallaudet University is attended by students from all over the world who are deaf or hard of hearing. It has been a college since 1864. The school is named after Thomas Hopkins Gallaudet, who lived next door to a deaf child named Alice Cogswell, and who traveled to Europe to learn about teaching deaf children. His son Edward helped to establish the university.

A B C D E F G H I J K L M N O P Q R S T U V W X Y Z

Holocaust Memorial Museum

It documents a time of dread
When crimes of hate left millions dead,
And teaches that what happened then
Must never come to pass again.

The Holocaust refers to the destruction of six million Jews by the Nazis and their followers in Europe between the years 1933 and 1945. Other individuals and groups in smaller numbers were also persecuted and suffered gravely during this time. The Holocaust Memorial Museum is dedicated to the memory of the Holocaust victims. The three main purposes of the museum are remembrance, education, and conscience.

Shortly after World War II, diplomats from Islamic countries built the Islamic Center to share their culture and religion with the United States. The mosque is the most important building in the center. It faces the holy city of Mecca in Saudi Arabia and is open to all.

Islamic Center

With minarets of soaring height
The mosque presents a striking sight.
Here those who practice Islam pray,
And those who wish to visit, may.

Jefferson Memorial

This peaceful monument reveres
A statesman, wise in many spheres,
Author of the Declaration,
And third head of our fledgling nation.

"The care of human life and happiness, and not their destruction, is the first and only legitimate object of good government."
—Thomas Jefferson

"The tree of liberty must be refreshed from time to time with the blood of patriots and tyrants."
—Thomas Jefferson

"I hold it, that a little rebellion, now and then, is a good thing. . . ."
—Thomas Jefferson

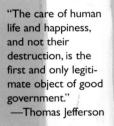

Thomas Jefferson
1743-1826

THE JEFFERSON MEMORIAL, WASHINGTON, D.C.

The Jefferson Memorial is modeled on a building in Rome called the Pantheon. Inscribed inside are several quotations from Jefferson's writings. The statue of Thomas Jefferson looks toward the White House.

MONTICELLO, CHARLOTTESVILLE, VIRGINIA

Jefferson loved to design buildings, including his own home, Monticello. The name means "little mountain."

THOMAS JEFFERSON, ESQ.

Jefferson had many acquaintances and friends, and wrote over 20,000 letters in his lifetime!

Thomas Jefferson was a man of many accomplishments: third president of the United States, author of the Declaration of Independence, architect, inventor, farmer, lawyer, violinist, and founder of the University of Virginia.

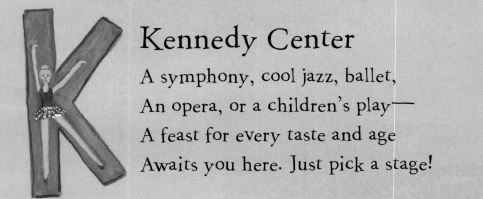

Kennedy Center

A symphony, cool jazz, ballet,
An opera, or a children's play—
A feast for every taste and age
Awaits you here. Just pick a stage!

The Kennedy Center was built as a living memorial to President John F. Kennedy, who loved and supported the arts. It is home to the National Symphony Orchestra, the Washington Opera, and the Washington Ballet. It hosts performances of ballet, opera, classical music, jazz, plays, and musical theater from all around the world.

"I am certain that after the dust of centuries has passed over our cities, we, too, will be remembered not for victories or defeats in battle or in politics, but for our contribution to the human spirit."
— John F. Kennedy

John F. Kennedy

An 8-foot bronze bust (head and neck) of President Kennedy looks over the Grand Foyer, which is one of the largest rooms in the world.

Harp

Triangle

Flutes

Clarinets

Trumpets

French horns

Timpani

Violins

Conductor

Cellos

Orchestra comes from ancient Greek. It was the section of the theater, between the stage and audience, where the musicians performed.

Lincoln Memorial

He ended slavery's abomination
And fought to reunite our nation.
His statue looks across the Mall;
His wise words stretch from wall to wall.

Abraham Lincoln, sixteenth president, was born in a log cabin in Kentucky on February 12, 1809.

Lincoln was fatally shot at Ford's Theatre by John Wilkes Booth on April 14, 1865.

Known as the Great Emancipator, Lincoln issued the Emancipation Proclamation to free the slaves. He led our country through the Civil War, preserving the Union.

The Lincoln Memorial was designed to look like the Parthenon, the most famous of ancient Greek temples.

The Gettysburg Address

Four score and seven years ago our fathers brought forth on this continent, a new nation, conceived in Liberty, and dedicated to the proposition that all men are created equal.

Now we are engaged in a great civil war, testing whether that nation or any nation so conceived and so dedicated, can long endure. We are met on a great battle-field of that war. We have come to dedicate a portion of that field, as a final resting place for those who here gave their lives that that nation might live. It is altogether fitting and proper that we should do this.

But, in a larger sense, we can not dedicate— we can not consecrate—we can not hallow— this ground. The brave men, living and dead, who struggled here, have consecrated it, far above our poor power to add or detract. The world will little note, nor long remember what we say here, but it can never forget what they did here. It is for us the living, rather, to be dedicated here to the unfinished work which they who fought here have thus far so nobly advanced. It is rather for us to be here dedicated to the great task remaining before us—that from these honored dead we take increased devotion to that cause for which they gave the last full measure of devotion—that we here highly resolve that these dead shall not have died in vain—that this nation, under God, shall have a new birth of freedom—and that government of the people, by the people, for the people, shall not perish from the earth.

The statue shows Lincoln as a tired but powerful man. One hand is clenched to show his strong will in keeping the nation together during the Civil War. The other hand is open to show that he was warm and caring.

Lincoln Memorial

Freer Gallery

Washington Monument

Metro stop

M SMITHSONIAN

Arthur M. Sackler Gallery

National Museum of African Art

Smithsonian Institution Building (The Castle)

Arts and Industries Building

Hirshhorn Museum and Sculpture Garden

National Air and Space Museum

The Mall

No cars allowed! Just trees for shade
And lots of space to promenade
Or skate or ride a wooden horse,
And visit the museums, of course!

National Museum of American History

On August 28, 1963, Dr. Martin Luther King, Jr., stood on the steps of the Lincoln Memorial. He made his "I Have a Dream" speech to about 250,000 people gathered in the Mall to support civil rights for all Americans.

The idea for the National Mall began when George Washington hired Pierre L'Enfant to design the new capital city of the United States. L'Enfant designed long, wide avenues and parklands as a central part of the city.

National Museum of Natural History

National Museums

Picassos, stegosaurus bones,
Tarantulas and precious stones,
Old Glory, giant squid, and more,
All send this message: "Come explore!"

National Gallery of Art

The first amendment to the U.S. Constitution gives all Americans freedom of speech. People from all over the country often join together at the Mall to speak out about things that are important to them.

Capitol

There are 897 steps inside that go all the way to the top. There's also an elevator!

Potomac River

Obelisk

Five hundred fifty-five feet high,
This structure aims straight for the sky,
Symbol of president number one
(And of our capital), Washington!

WASHINGTON
MONUMENT

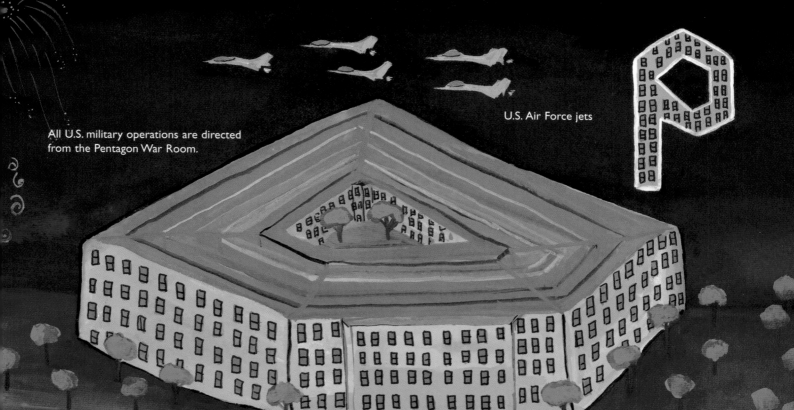

U.S. Air Force jets

All U.S. military operations are directed from the Pentagon War Room.

Pentagon

Headquarters for the high command,
From here their strategies are planned,
And our armed forces are directed
To keep the U.S. well protected.

The Pentagon is the headquarters of the Department of Defense and the Army, Navy, Marines, and Air Force. Named for its five-sided shape, the Pentagon is like a small city—26,000 people work there, there are 17.5 miles of hallway, and it covers 29 acres. Five U.S. Capitol buildings could fit inside!

Dumbarton Oaks

Q Street

There's lots to see in this locale:
Quaint shops, the C & O Canal,
The Old Stone House, Dumbarton, too,
Are found on streets from "M" to "Q."

Georgetown was named after King George II
of England. It was built on land owned by
George Beall and George Gordon and was
visited frequently by George Washington.

Wisconsin Avenue

31st Street

In the nineteenth century,
barges were pulled up and
down the canal by mules.

C & O Canal

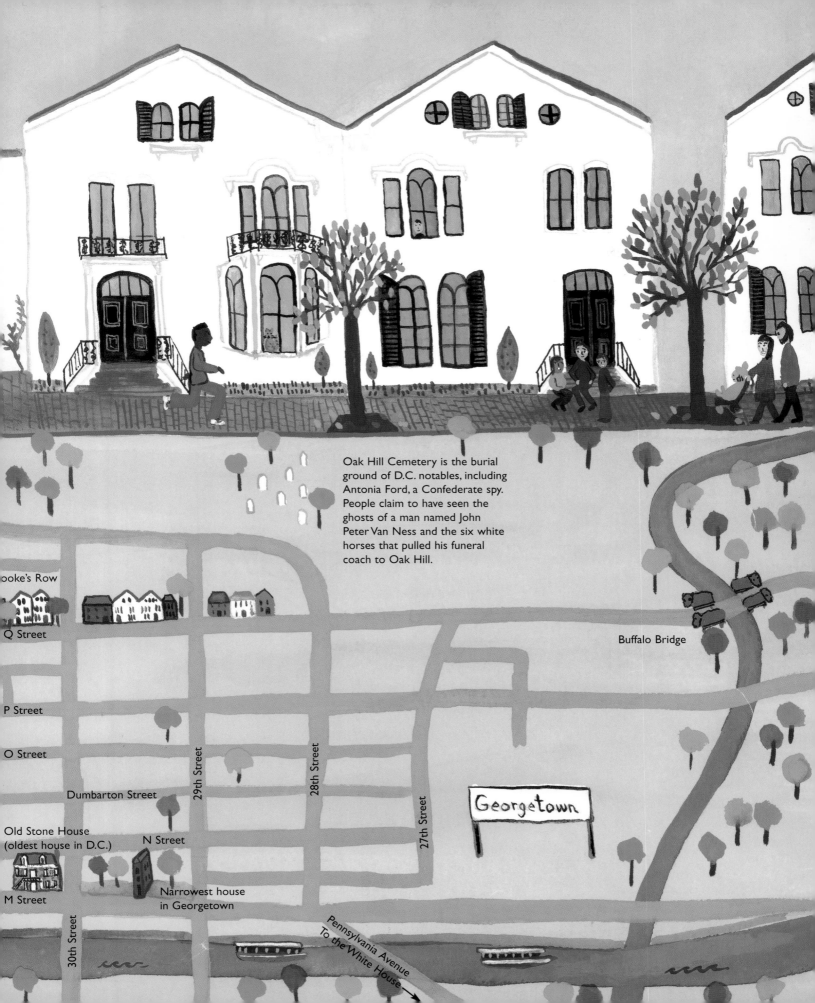

Oak Hill Cemetery is the burial ground of D.C. notables, including Antonia Ford, a Confederate spy. People claim to have seen the ghosts of a man named John Peter Van Ness and the six white horses that pulled his funeral coach to Oak Hill.

Cooke's Row

Q Street

Buffalo Bridge

P Street

O Street

29th Street

28th Street

Dumbarton Street

27th Street

Georgetown

Old Stone House
(oldest house in D.C.)

N Street

Narrowest house
in Georgetown

M Street

30th Street

Pennsylvania Avenue
To the White House →

Roosevelt Memorial

A president called FDR
Was not afraid of want or war.
He guided our great country through
Depression years and World War II.

"I pledge you, I pledge myself, to a new deal for the American people."
—Franklin Delano Roosevelt

THE ONLY THING WE HAVE TO FEAR IS FEAR ITSELF

FIRST TERM 1933-1937

When Franklin Delano Roosevelt, known as FDR, first ran for president, times were very hard. One third of all Americans had no jobs. FDR promised that things would get better, and his plan was called the New Deal.

Although many people still stood in long lines for a little food, FDR's New Deal created many new jobs. People built bridges, buildings, and dams. They painted murals and houses and wrote books.

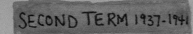

SECOND TERM 1937-1941

FDR gave weekly radio talks called Fireside Chats to let Americans know he was working hard for them.

"We have faith that future generations will know that here, in the middle of the twentieth century, there came a time when men of good will found a way to unite, and produce, and fight to destroy the forces of ignorance, and intolerance, and slavery, and war."
—Franklin Delano Roosevelt

Fala was FDR's little black Scottish terrier. He went everywhere with FDR, ate his meals in the president's study, and slept every night in a chair at the foot of the president's bed.

During FDR's third term, countries in Europe and Asia were fighting the Second World War, but the United States stayed neutral. Then on December 7, 1941, Japan attacked the U.S. Navy's ships in Pearl Harbor, Hawaii, and FDR led the United States into war.

I HATE

WAR

THIRD TERM 1941-1945

FREEDOM FROM FEAR
FREEDOM FROM WANT
FREEDOM OF WORSHIP
FREEDOM OF SPEECH

FDR was elected to a fourth term as president—more terms than any other president had served. However, he had a stroke and died soon after his election; his vice president, Harry S. Truman, became president. The nation mourned the loss of its great leader.

Eleanor Roosevelt was FDR's wife. She helped the poor and worked for civil rights. World leaders respected her so much that they often came to her for advice.

FOURTH TERM 1945

Supreme Court

Nine judges on this highest court
Hear cases of supreme import,
Oath-bound to reach a resolution
Upholding our Constitution.

Before the justices sit down, the marshal chants: "The honorable, the Chief Justice and the Associate Justices of the Supreme Court of the United States. Oyez! Oyez! Oyez! All persons having business before the Honorable, the Supreme Court of the United States, are admonished to draw near and give their attention, for the Court is now sitting. God save the United States and this Honorable Court!"

John Paul Stevens

Antonin Scalia

David H. Souter

Ruth Bader Ginsburg

On Monday, Tuesday, and Wednesday, visitors may be present in the court while it is sitting.

The Constitution says the United States Supreme Court is the highest court in the land. The justices are appointed by the president and must be approved by the Senate. They are appointed for life.

William H. Rehnquist

Sandra Day O'Connor

Anthony M. Kennedy

Clarence Thomas

Stephen G. Breyer

The Court has *sittings*, when the justices hear cases and give opinions, and *recesses*, when they write opinions. Both last about two weeks.

EQUAL JUSTICE UNDER LAW

When a case is argued before the Court, each side is allowed to speak for only 30 minutes and may be interrupted by a justice at any time. The justices may hear up to 24 cases at one sitting.

Tomb of the Unknowns

Within a stately tomb of stone
Three soldiers rest, their names unknown.
Each perished in a different fight;
Now sentries guard them day and night.

HERE RESTS IN
HONORED GLORY
AN AMERICAN
SOLDIER
KNOWN BUT TO GOD

The soldiers buried in the Tomb of the Unknowns lost their lives fighting for the United States in World War I, World War II, and the Korean War. No one knows their names.

Sentinels guard the tomb at all times.

The Tomb of the Unknowns is in Arlington National Cemetery, across the Potomac River from Washington.

An eternal flame burns at John F. Kennedy's grave in the cemetery.

The Iwo Jima Memorial was erected in memory of those who gave their lives during this World War II battle in the Pacific.

The barrel-vaulted ceiling is 96 feet high.

Statues of Roman soldiers stand guard on the balcony around the Main Hall.

Union Station

This grand train station, once ignored,
Has been most carefully restored.
No longer just a traveler's stop,
It's now a place to dine and shop.

Union Station opened in 1907 on the edge of a muddy shanty-town called Swampoodle.

Along with train travelers, many people come to Union Station for its restaurants, shops, and movie theaters. It has more visitors than any other site in D.C.

Vietnam Veterans Memorial

Our troops fought there at awful cost
With almost sixty thousand lost.
Today we walk beside the wall
To read each name and mourn them all.

On the wall are inscribed the names of Americans who died or were declared missing in the Vietnam War. They are listed in the order in which the men and women died or were declared missing.

"This memorial is for those who have died, and for us to remember them."
—Maya Ying Lin, designer of Vietnam Veterans Memorial Wall

Before the memorial was built, a contest was held to choose a design. The judges were artists and architects. They looked at designs sent in by 1,421 people. Maya Lin was the winner. At the time she was a 21-year-old college student.

White House

A symbol of democracy,
This house belongs to you and me,
And each new U.S. president
May take a turn as resident.

The private living quarters of the president and his family make up only a small portion of the total space.

President's Bedroom

Study

State Dining Room

Red Room

Blue Room

Some federal employees have offices in the White House.

Map Room

Diplomatic Reception Room

The White House has six floors, 132 rooms, over 30 bathrooms, 147 windows, and 3 elevators. It is called the White House because of the whitewash paint used to protect the sandstone blocks that form the walls.

During the War of 1812, British troops marched on the White House to torch it. The building was badly burned and would have been destroyed if not for a sudden thunderstorm quenching the flames.

A quote from John Adams, the first president to live in the White House, is engraved in the State Dining Room: "I pray Heaven to Bestow the Best of Blessings on This House and on All that shall hereafter inhabit it. May none but Honest and Wise Men ever rule under this roof."

Green Room

East Room

China Room

Vermeil Room

The Secret Service protects the White House around the clock.

Two-toed sloth

Xanthosoma

Poison arrow frog

Iguana

Titi monkey

Yellow-spotted
sidenecked turtle

X
Xanthosoma

Y
Yellow-Spotted
Sidenecked
Turtle

Z
Zygopetalon

Scarlet macaw

Y

Piranha

Zygopetalon

National Zoo
Within a forest, steamy-hot,
Live Xanthosoma, Yellow-spot,
Blue frog and fish, and monkey, too—
It's Amazonia, at the Zoo!

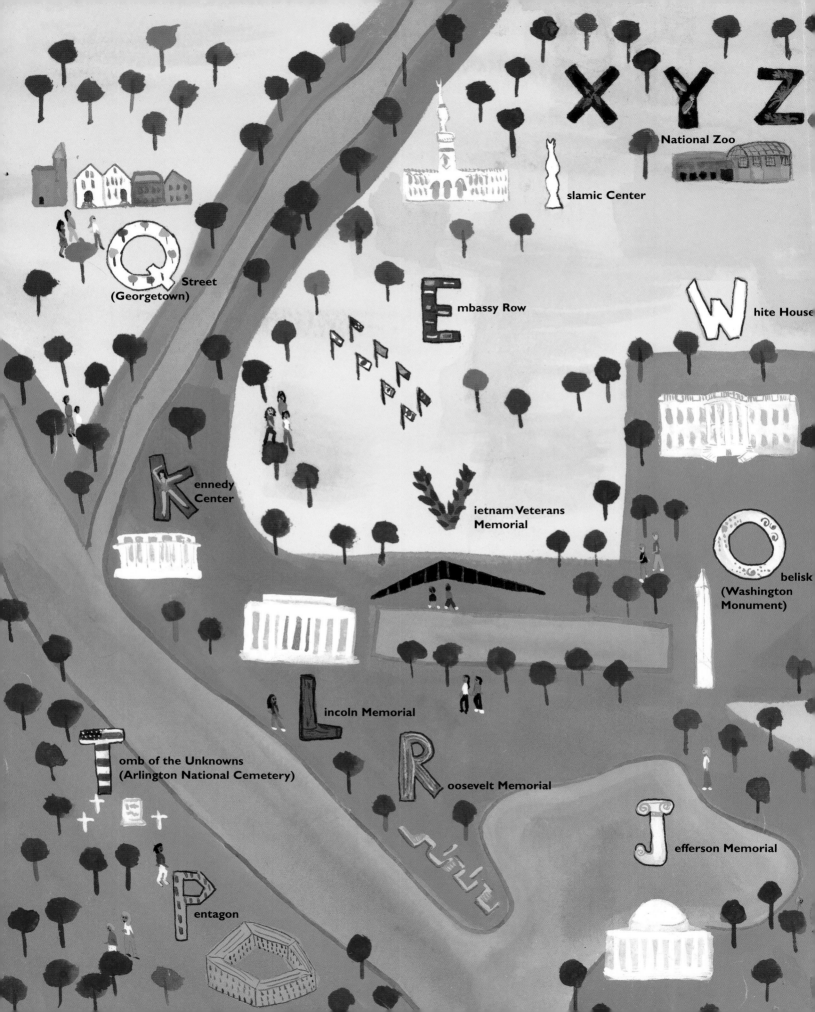

X Y Z

National Zoo

slamic Center

Q Street
(Georgetown)

E mbassy Row

W hite House

K ennedy
Center

V ietnam Veterans
Memorial

O belisk
(Washington
Monument)

L incoln Memorial

R oosevelt Memorial

J efferson Memorial

T omb of the Unknowns
(Arlington National Cemetery)

P entagon